A New Hunger

A NEW HUNGER

LAURE-ANNE BOSSELAAR

AUSABLE PRESS
2007

Cover art: "The Bad Sower" by Gustave van de Woestijne
1908. Oil on panel. 56 x 46 cm.
Private collection, Antwerp, Belgium

Design and composition by Ausable Press
The type is Granjon with Trajan titling.
Cover design by Rebecca Soderholm
Author photo by Star Black

Published by
Ausable Press
1026 Hurricane Road
Keene, NY 12942
www.ausablepress.org

Distributed to the trade by
Perseus Distribution Services
1094 Flex Drive
Jackson, TN 38301
Toll-free: 800-283-3572
Fax: 800-351-5073

First edition, third printing

Library of Congress Cataloging-in-Publication Data

Bosselaar, Laure-Anne, 1943—
A new hunger / Laure-Anne Bosselaar.—1st ed.
p. cm.
ISBN-13: 978-1-931337-32-8 (alk. paper)
ISBN-10: 1-931337-32-2 (alk. paper)
I. Title.

PS3552.O772N49 2007
811'.54—dc22
2006030588

for Thomas Lux

A NEW HUNGER

AGAINST AGAIN
Against Again *1*

THE RIVER'S MOUTH, THE BOAT, THE UNDERTOW
The River's Mouth, the Boat, the Undertow *17*

A NEW HUNGER
Memory Mall *33*

Stillbirth *35*

March Chimes *36*

Elegy *37*

Bus Stop *38*

Counted *39*

Swallowing *41*

Garage Sale *43*

The Want for a Cloud *44*

On a Bench by the Hudson *46*

Man at the Museum of Modern Art *48*

Birthday *50*

It Had to Be You *52*

Awe *54*

Note Slipped Under His Door *56*

At Savage River Lodge *57*

Friends *60*

Night *62*

Notes & Acknowledgments *67*

Against Again

AGAINST AGAIN

The train bursts out of the tunnel into a New Jersey sunset.
A gray haze looms over smoke stacks and storage tanks.

The man next to me reads the paper; he smells of plastic or glue,
and I'm astounded again at those transitory

intimacies we share with strangers: the man's
shoulder, hip and thigh against mine —

even our breaths are in sync —

yet I know nothing of him, and he nothing of me
but my own smell perhaps, which he'll forget even

before stepping off at his station. It will be Rahway —

raw way —

but I don't know that yet.

*

I don't open the book I hold in my lap: I'm reading faces
around me, a jumble of wonder

and furious exhaustion,

bare, hard features, framed and drafted by birth
toward this commute — since when and to where?—

each face naked with braveness.

Even this small child, harnessed into a dirty stroller:
all she can see are legs. For her,

this train is packed with pants, belts, zippers and shoes —

and look at her face: already courageous, defeated,
and old with it.

*

All I have left of my mother's face is her profile:
the way her face turned away, always —

and how swiftly that profile gave way
to the back of her neck,

and the perfect curls she set there.

For she set them there, each morning, with willful seduction.

I spent my childhood clinging to an image of her face
bending toward mine.

She was the one kissing me on the lips when,
some nights, I kissed myself in a mirror. I swear,

once, the mirror breathed Chanel No. 5
back into my mouth.

*

The only thing that clung to me was her perfume
the first time she left me at a nunnery. I didn't look at her:

I was staring at my new black shoes— and at two
other pairs of feet: mother's in tan ostrich pumps,
with silk bows and stilettos,

the other caught in thick-soled sandals scarcely
showing under a heavy, dark hem.

When the stilettos
left, I couldn't

lift my head. It wasn't because of the shoes,
or the smell of cabbage smothering mother's perfume,

but because I was turning deaf. Not to Antwerp's
streetcars, or the rain tearing at the windows —

I could no longer hear mother's voice,

yet my suitcase was still

there, on the marble floor.

*

The infant in the stroller whimpers shy vowels.
Her mother flips pages of a magazine. The child whines

again, frets, cranes her neck to see her mother's
face, but the stroller's

black hood is in the way.

The man next to me sighs, uncrosses and crosses
his legs. His hip, for an instant,

away from mine. But then it's back again,

against me. Against again.

And that smell of glue.

*

Nun's faces replaced mother's: thickset in wimples
so tight the wrinkles and jowls were pushed forward
like the skin of old fruit —

faces without foreheads, ears or necks.

Without curls.

I was only four, so that first day, when the nun

carrying my suitcase opened the door
to the dormitory and walked me between

two endless rows of beds,

I clung to her hand and believed her
when she said mother would come

back for me soon.

*

That first night: sixty-four new faces, sixty-four
pairs of ravenous eyes stared at me.

Long, dormitory rows of beds. Tall red brick walls. High
windows. Curtains caught in wrought iron rings.

Sixty-four beds, sixty-six chairs, one between each bed,
plus two extra for a nun at each end of the room.

Then years of nights.

Curtain rings chinking shut.

A few murmurs. Hushes.

The shush and rustle of small bodies
settling into sheets,

the low lament of bed springs,

and nights of silence — faintly alive
with the tinkle of the nun's metal knitting needles

and a new scent that drifted and curled
between our beds like a whisper: the oily,

sharp scent we all shared: *Savon de Marseille:*

large bricks of green soap Sister Eucharistine
cut into slices with a cheese cutter and distributed on Mondays.

They were to last until Sunday nights.

I learned to wash with water every
other day, so the slivers would last.

We all did that.

*

A girl in one of the end beds — Vivianne —
coughed and wheezed for weeks until we were told

she left for a better place in her Father's garden.

Hannah, to my right, had a harelip and pinched everyone.

The girl to my left cried often, sucking her pillow's corners:

Marieke.

Marieke and Hannah. Vivianne.

Sister Brigitte.
Sister Kelleen.
Sister Bénédicte.

Mother Saint-Pierre.
Mother Superior.

Mother
gone.

And in storage, my suitcase.

Inside it,
my name bracelet and stuffed dog.

On the dormitory chairs, our uniforms
neatly folded. Nothing else. We couldn't
own anything from home.

But the chairs — the high-backed oak chairs — were
ours, labeled with our names, in black cursives.

*

Who knows what became of the other chair, the one my mother
flung, years later, missing me at first — down on my knees,
arms over my head — but she hurled it again. It hit my neck.

I had spilled ink on her rug.

She was beautiful, violently beautiful and blond.

Her laughter — a child's — sprinkled the rooms
with prettiness, the way sparkles skittered on walls
when her rings caught the sun.

Someone had died in the family that week.
A taxi drove me home.

Father smelled of cologne. He smoked
Chesterfields from a golden holder. Ashes fluttered —
tiny moths — on his lapels.

Mother wore a Brussels lace veil and elbow-length gloves
closed by long rows of tiny black pearls like glimmering rosaries.

She dressed me in a blue velvet coat, with black fur
pompoms as buttons, urging me to be polite and say

thank you if someone spoke to me.

At the funeral, she whispered how *adoringly* the priest's
alb had been embroidered, how *delicately refined* it was —

and hours later, I had spilled ink on her rug.
Ink.

*

And it comes back to me: how *adoringly* I'd breathe —

in sync with her —

the few times she held me. Soothed, sated with her perfume,
my face in the curls she poised on her neck,

I felt chosen — *possessed* almost — by un-brokenness.

Not innocence or forgiveness. Un-brokenness.

And for weeks I existed, almost whole, after she
dropped me off at the convent again.

I waited for a letter, card, or call.
Months of waiting.

I still have the handkerchiefs she gave me, seven of them,
each delicately embroidered with the name of a day:

Lundi, Mardi, Mercredi . . .

The nuns allowed me to keep them:
handkerchiefs were useful. Handkerchiefs served.

*

Years of days, also.

Matins' incense tracing letters in the air.

Boiled fish and rutabaga. Stewed horsemeat.

Boiled beets we'd rub on our lips and cheeks
like make-up, and were punished for it.

*

Beatings and punishments:

closed-fist punches to the back of our heads:
they didn't leave bruises. Kicks in the back of the knees
until they buckled.

Gravel in our palms, scrapes on our legs
Sister Cecilia dabbed with Mercurochrome.

*

And silences.

Silence in the refectory, silence in the halls,
at mass, at wash-sinks, in study hall.

Silences so long I coughed
to break them.

Winters so sunless I prayed
to the moon to warm us.

Months between postcards from Baden-Baden, Florence, Shanghai,

with only Father's four, spiked, green-inked letters
"Papa" under her blue *"Maman"* —

the blue ink I had spilled on her rug.

*

And springs — bright with Easter colors. Gold-waxed
refectory tables, dozens of honey-colored wicker baskets

brimming with eggs we painted
for prisoners and the poor.

Knitting and embroidery classes.

Years of knitting socks
for prisoners and the poor.
Gray with black borders.
Black with grey.

And Kristien, some nights, who slipped into my bed
to hold me, pressing my palms against her face,
kissing them as I kissed the back of her soap-smelling hands —
calling them *Maman*.

*

Then in June the linden tree bloomed, the air

fervent with its perfume.

We helped novices stretch sheets under the tree,
shook its limbs, hanging from them, laughing,
bouncing, screaming

as we harvested pillows of gold and green: a smell

so sweet the breeze — drunk with it — strewed sunlight,
bees and leaves all around us.

Skirts billowed, novices twittered under the tree
like hens around their chicks.

Sunday nights in summer, we drank linden
tea, its soothing, blond aroma curling in my mouth.

*

Stations have come and gone. The man next to me
sleeps. One hand on his thigh, the other on his paper,

palm up. His fingers twitch faintly, and I suddenly
long for that hand, yet just as suddenly need it to close,
to flip back, palm down, and stop being so intimately

open there, vulnerable and foreign.

*

I'm sick of this train, the fleeting faces, the man's
frayed sleeve

and unavailable body half fused to mine,

its smell fading
away — it too turning

away from the quiet chaos I'm made of,
the vortex I come from —

odors, profiles, chairs, soap, kisses, hands —

schedules and stations swept into the past,
lost among smoke stacks, storage tanks

and other trains. All that wandering.

*

The train slows again. The man stirs,
rubs his face and neck with both hands,

stands, folds his paper neatly,
and leaves it on the seat.
I don't move, don't dare look up
and sit there, staring at my shoes

as I feel him disappear — my whole body
feels him leave.

*

That was it.

A transitory nearness,
a transit story.

And always this hunger,
an exhausted longing —

the wait and the weight.

THE RIVER'S MOUTH, THE BOAT, THE UNDERTOW

THE RIVER'S MOUTH, THE BOAT, THE UNDERTOW

Letting go of it — that first balloon — remember?
A dot lost in the air, a voice consoling:
It's *just* a balloon, you'll get another one.

Too soon you're the one saying: It's *only* a glove,
dog, lover or job — as you move on, just one of the many
bending over another job, dog, love. But the balloon:
how suddenly it was gone.

How suddenly it was lost. How swiftly hushed
the crying child. How resiliently we adjust
to black dots in the sky: only dust,

swallows, pock marks on the moon. Or planes,
but flying high enough, away enough. Or just
snow, the voice on the radio consoling: only
a blizzard on its way.

A blizzard on its way, and the pain squalls are back
again. She misses him — although what mars
most is no longer the missing, but how

blunt the grief has become. How seeing a man today,
with the same cowlick he had, there, by his left
temple, brought gratitude — and no longer pain.
The heart refusing one more stab of it.

His heart refusing one more stab, had stopped. He was found
leaning against a tree, frozen. His skis a few feet below. Not a red
trace in the snow, just a bruise by his temple, where his head

hit the tree. At the hospital, left alone with him at last,
she lifts the sheet, his gown, takes off her clothes and lies
against him, her face in his neck. She hears nothing. Then,
the wing-whistle of birds taking flight.

Ah, those wing-whistles of birds taking flight! No painter
could evoke such sound. No music describe his mother's
glance, at once rising sun and Crow Moon. No clay, wood

or marble render the perfume in his mistress's hair. No
camera could ever capture his *oeuvre!* But poetry, poetry
did it all . . . Thus muses the celebrated poet on a bench,
a moleskin notebook in his lap.

In his moleskin notebook, he underlines the word
marvelous. Reads it to himself: "Marvelous, the odors/
in my lover's hair." He loves that dactyl: *mar*velous.

Had it been sung that well before? Wasn't it Baudelaire?
But who, he asks his muse, who'll be the *most*
immortal of us all? *The clouds,* she whispers,
over there . . . over there . . . the marvelous clouds.

Pierre would quote: *Là-bas... là-bas... les merveilleux nuages...*
while he painted the King's palace gates in Brussels.
She brought him lunch, sat by him on the sidewalk.

They'd sing Jacques Brel together: *Ne me quitte pas...*
May of '61: they were seventeen. Pierre's mother cleaned
the Opera dressing rooms at night. When she left for work,
they ran up to his attic room to make love.

In his attic room, they made love, read Gide and Goethe.
He'd become a poet, she the next Lotte Lenya. The army
drafted him that fall. Then, his letters: write, please,

I miss you. She couldn't. Not after what she'd let the doctor do
to her so he'd take care of her problem for free. All these years
she kept the last picture Pierre sent: awkward in his uniform,
his forehead to the window. The landscape frozen.

A man's forehead to a window. The landscape frozen.
He is old, suddenly. Broken. His last passion, over. Leaving
that woman made it so: he knows this with glacial certainty.

He'll turn to books, crank the stereo in the head-sets,
let it choke his wife's silences and the deafening
cell phone: the other woman calling him, calling still.
Outside, the first snow. Effacing, persistent.

Effacing, a persistent snow. Her husband reads upstairs,
the silence barely broken by his phone's shy chimes —
left unanswered. Over at last, his long nights at work:

the endless meetings, business trips. She hears his study floor
creak — he must be walking to the window again —
she loves how he takes time to day-dream now, and how
he listens to his music, eyes closed, hands joined.

She listens to music, eyes closed, hands joined, headset
lost in thick black curls. A button on her jean jacket reads
Still Against The War. Next to her on the bus,

a small boy frowns, mouthing something to his plastic
police car. Now and then he looks up at an older woman
who has been staring at them for a while. That's
all I'll ever know about them.

All I'll ever know is that we traveled a few blocks together
and nothing happened. What thoughts they had, what
the child mouthed, what music the woman listened to —

insignificant. Right? It was only *me* thinking the boy wanted
to shoot the class bully from that cop car, right? Or imagining
the older woman was a racist, and the other a dreamer.
What would you have seen? What would you have thought?

What would you have seen? What would you have thought
watching those two men crossing the Brooklyn Bridge, *shrill
shirts ballooning,* trying to understand each other, hands

swooping up the air like gulls. That the poets *gave each other
wisdom or love or even a good time* isn't the point — it's that
no one crossing them on the bridge that day recognized them,
or stopped in awe to watch Crane and Lorca walk by.

No one noticed Crane and Lorca walk by, they weren't stars,
presidents, pitchers or popes after all — only two men standing
with empty hands in the murmur of the rivers' mouth.

*The two greatest poetic geniuses alive meet, and what
happens?* What did they see, what did they talk about,
feel, or think then, as around them the air, clouds and
waters went on shuffling chance and light?

Waters went on shuffling chance and light as the boy
jumped into the river. He had come home from school
that day with a drawing for his dad and found him

overdosed on the couch. The Czech have a word for what
drowned the boy. For what it is that guts a woman's belly
long after an abortion; a word for what hurts, exactly,
when a sheet is pulled over a child, mother, soldier.

In sheets pulled over a child or soldier, there is *litost*.
At the auction of his tractor, *litost* plows a farmer's heart.
In bombs strapped to a terrorist's chest or in the guns

pointed at him — *litost*. Kundera tells us it's untranslatable,
that we have no word for this in English. But here's the point —
what if we did? Would a word make such pain more tolerable?
As if language could help.

As if a language could help her survive, the ten-year-old
decides to invent a new one that won't have words for what
she fears or sees, or who and what she must forget —

except for *mother,* and *father.* Except for that, she will
never speak or understand German again. She'll make
up new words each day, repeat them, learn them
by heart — like songs.

A new language like a song she'll keep singing to herself
the way her parents did on the train that brought them here.
But without words for *home, Jew, or Treblinka.*

She'll make up a new time also: no hours, nights, winters,
only *now* and *soon,* so that when the train will come
to take her home again with her parents, it'll be all at once
now *and* soon.

And soon — sure enough — his wife's hand moves
up his thigh to his groin, gently. Fourteen years of this:
her incessant gentleness, and his trying and

failing, failing again to respond to her, or find
a better job, be there for their son, keep up
with the mortgage — and now her hand
moves away.

She moves away from him, limp with failure,
his forearm over his eyes. Would you recognize them
standing in line at the bank, posing in magazines,

smiling at you from home videos? Look: she holds
the cake, he blows the candles and waves at you,
blowing kisses to the past, present and future
of what he fears most.

What he feared most was not death, but to lose wonder.
Death had taught him his first suck, step, words. She
had been his first tango partner, lover, shot of gin;

she coached him on how to stomach longing — she bore
his mother's face, her voice and distance. But it was
on his own, a child still, that he had learned wonder: like
a thief who got away, he stole it from a shore.

He stole it from the sand: a small shell, dull
as the world around him. In the dank stealth of his room
he opened it: the shape of a heart now, it held

the taste of salt on skin, the colors of sails, peach
blossoms in spring. What it no longer held was a void
familiar to him. But what had remained was wonder:
an emptiness beginning to stir.

Daybreak. An emptiness beginning to stir. Less
than a breath, air drafts ripple the water. Cattail seeds
teeter and fall. The color of haze, a crane

lifts from the reeds. Hands in the bib of his overalls,
an old black man stands by the water. Dragonflies
flutter and yaw. A web tugs at a twig —
the man bends to look at it.

He bends toward her, his white-striped spider
in her messy web. He spent hours once, watching her
feast on a caterpillar. He picks a loosestrife leaf,

slips it between his lips, walks away, whistling. Hours later,
the great wrack: trucks, tractors, and a Caterpillar crane
lifting a billboard — *Green Pond Mall Opening Soon* —
against the blank, tin sky.

In a blank, tin sky: one sparrow. And you, love,
in the pauses between footsteps in our house.
Or in silences so unyielding I can hear you swallow.

You and I in the stoop's cracks where weeds grow. Inside
night's cravings, and beyond them. In our house-
key's clatter, the porch-light's glow. And on bills:
our names, together, behind those lucid windows.

Your name and mine in those windows, and in the name
we would have given our child. (Inside the blank,
tin sky, love — that one sparrow).

Into again. Into tomorrow. Then, toward the river's
mouth, the boat, the undertow. Within the stillness
that will follow. Toward that also — toward
the letting go.

A New Hunger

MEMORY MALL

　　　　Funneled into, tunnelled
toward the past's underground:

lives, loves — millennia of them.

　　　　Cemeteries, mass graves, urns.
Photo albums, memorials, memoirs:

all clogged with indispensable souls.

　　　　If that's too abstract, think
your first love, your neighbor's dog,

the stone carver's son, or Rainer Maria Rilke —

　　　　all equally fated, standing in line for,
or already crowding, memory's mall.

I long for that promiscuity: dead gods,

　　　　scholars, cops and whores equally
longing for remembrance, selling

their tricks to nothing but bones and dust.

　　　　I've prayed for death, ardently.
And ardently pray

to be forgiven each plea, fearing the black draft

       might pull the ones I love
into that vortex too —

a siren song we try to sing louder than —

       but our tune nothing more
than cinders turning to stone: a rock

no memory, love or god can ever roll back.

STILLBIRTH

On a platform, I heard someone call out your name:
No, Laetitia, no.
It wasn't my train — the doors were closing,
But I rushed in, searching for your face.

But no Laetitia. No.
No one in that car could have been you,
but I rushed in, searching for your face:
no longer an infant. A woman now, blond, thirty-two.

No one in that car could have been you.
Laetitia-Marie was the name I had chosen.
No longer an infant. A woman now, blond, thirty-two:
I sometimes go months without remembering you.

Laetitia-Marie was the name I had chosen:
I was told not to look. Not to get attached —
I sometimes go months without remembering you.
Some griefs bless us that way, not asking much space.

I was told not to look. Not to get attached.
It wasn't my train — the doors were closing.
Some griefs bless us that way, not asking much space.
On a platform, I heard someone calling your name.

MARCH CHIMES

Day dithers, no wind or breeze, and light
so drab it could be dawn or dusk.

Winter recedes to nothing again, what's
left of snow dull. Silent sparrows, still pond.

I throw a coat over my shoulders, step
out. How barrenness weighs!

I pick up a stone, hurl it at the chimes.
Their notes seed the silence, ripples

skitter in the pond, sparrows prattle,
there's a breath caught in the highest tree,

and suddenly all this nothingness is alive
with possibility, like the day I knew

I was pregnant with you.
And I remember it now — that void

inside me when nothing stirred, nothing
moved, my body between seasons, drawing

trust from patience and patience from hope.

for Maelle

ELEGY

The past lies in the swath I left
crossing a summer meadow in Belgium.

I longed to see my old house one
last time, and crossed the field at dawn.

Some grasses lifted their heads
after my passage — wild chamomile and chervil —

but the touch-me-not lay crushed.
I found nothing there I wanted to bring back

and no one was left to see me turn away.

BUS STOP

Sullen, stubborn sleet all day.
Traffic jammed on Sixth. We cram
the shelter, soaked strangers, shivering,
straining to see the bus,

except for a man next to me,
dialing his cell-phone. He hunches,
pulls his parka's collar over it, talks
slow and low:

It's Daddy, honey. You do? Me too.
Ask Mommy if I can come see you now.
Oh, okay. Sunday. Bye. Me too. Bye.

He snaps the phone shut,
holds it to his cheek, staring at nothing.
Dusk stains the sleet, minutes slush by.

When we board the bus,
he's still pressing the phone to his cheek.

COUNTED

In the park — while her mother
and another woman hold each other and kiss —
a three year-old counts pencils in a box:

one, two, four, five, seven . . .

She has already lived long
enough for shadows to pencil her in, already

knows hunger and the long
ache to be held

while all along the insatiable Counter
has held her: each one of her frowns,
each breath

while all along spring
is pastelling everything —

the park, counting child, kissing
women and city dogs. They yap,
unleashed in the gravel and reek of *their*
fenced-in park.

Balls and sticks fly,
are caught,
fly, are lost —

and none of this matters less or more than any
other seasons, kisses or shadows:

> tall ones cast by buildings
> (fencing in the park that
> fences in children
> and fenced-in dogs)

or the dun shadows thrown by the EXIT signs
on each floor of every building
in this heaving, hungry city.

Faces I'll never see or see
again — all of us counted,
caught, and penciled in:

> *one, two, four, five, seven . . .*

SWALLOWING

Swallow that, the mother orders, *swallow that
now.* Child begging *don't leave again, don't go.*

And the mother: *Swallow that.*

The child does. Good child, obedient one.
Learns ways to swallow better by counting

tiles on the bathroom wall until the sobs
shrivel. Imagines someone pushed from a building:

whose body, how that body, how long and loud
it would fall. Pictures mother *and* child — their bodies,

theirs together makes the swallowing easier —
how long and loud then the sirens and bells.

In church, the mother's clench on the growing
child's shoulder: *Sing, child. Sing louder.*

And the child does. Becomes good at it.

Bellows hymns, swallows more, steals
torch songs from stores —

don't leave me, baby, please don't go —
blasts them on the radio, earphones deafening in subways,

streets, alone in bed — deaf now to sirens, bells,
and phones ringing, voices begging *don't leave me*

again, don't go — deaf to all calls.
The heart swallowing, parched and dumb.

GARAGE SALE

I sold her bed for a song.
A song of yearning like an orphan's.
Or the one knives carve into bread.

But the un-broken bread
song too. For the song that a river
sings to the ferryman's oars — with

that dread in it.
For a threadbare tune: garroted,
chest-choked, cheap. A sparrow's,

beggar's, a foghorn's call.
For the kind of song only morning
can slap on love-stained sheets —

that's what I sold my mother's
bed for. The one she died in. Sold it
for a song.

THE WANT FOR A CLOUD

Another morning — and your name still
slices into me. There's no simile for this,

or metaphor about how sharp this is,
how dead you are. I'm afraid

I'm getting better at shrugging you away
each day, always at the same time,

when the city starts its cheap music,
belting the usual off-tune torch songs.

That impulse to go to the window to look at
anything — a man bolting a sign to a wall,

another taking a break in his junk
of a truck, thermos sticky with fingerprints.

This hunger to be distracted from thinking
of you — the want for a cloud, call, or a friend's

small tragedies to stop me from remembering
you. Is that when one begins to die?

When the slipknot you thought would never
let go of your throat feels looser? And when it does,

and you're secretly relieved — is that a sign?
And which of us exactly is it who is dying?

for Eric

ON A BENCH BY THE HUDSON

Behind me, concrete dumping, steel
slamming and curses echo from Ground Zero.

Before me what I come to see, but never
do, that place in the water where silent, invisible

and drowned, there is a perennial whirl — where
is it? — a swirl in the river where it ends its journey,

takes water and wrecks into the sea.

That precise place (or is it a moment?)
that you or I will never see: a sweet-salted swell

made of what is swallowed, dies, yet flows on,
flows into what it will become — both waters

mingled there — neither river nor sea,
but suspended, exquisitely, for an instant.

Then, the great ocean.

*

And this bench I keep coming back to.
Where others also come and go, their presence

a whirl in the air when they leave, before
I come to breathe in the city's swells,

watching the Hudson rush — an ashen estuary —
skyscrapers and ships dragged in its ripples.

Look at me sitting here, speaking softly to
myself in a language that isn't even mine,

staring at a dying river as if I could catch
a truth behind it,

lost in my journey away from my country,

my children facing other seas, and my pulse
a swirl, invisible, drowned —

    small beat, rush, sweet salt.

MAN AT THE MUSEUM OF MODERN ART

Whose name will be on his lips when he
dies? Whose body (weight, skin, fervors of it)

will he remember? Who was his first
ugliness? What his first treason?

He won't stop walking, doesn't look at
anything, wanders from room to escalator,

hall to other space — for an hour now —
carrying that plastic bag, a thick hardcover

askew in it. Why do I follow him? What
makes me do that, so often, in streets or

subways even, getting off before my stop
to follow a man, woman, couple?

Yesterday, on a park bench, I listened long
to the plucked, hushed vowels of two

women — who spoke a language I didn't
understand — their voices so drained I felt

hatred for something I couldn't name — and
still can't. It isn't *life* or *fate* or —

*

But this man today, with his knitted
scarf and old brown shoes in this insufferably

civilized place — it's Larry I see, Larry Levis:
his casual gestures, that staring-beyond

schism in his gaze, the head always tilted back or
away too much. I would have stalked

him too from subway to street, bench to bus,
wanting answers then turning away.

What else can I do but turn away
as I did from my own first ugliness:

hiding my face in my arm to
stop seeing Hannah's gaze — we were only six

and I was already evil. I can't forget her,
Hannah the hare-lip.

How horror stalks us — as desire does,
or love. Or hunger.

What answers do I want from this man
lost in a museum?

Whose name will be on my lips when I die?

BIRTHDAY

When winds whet their edges
on the angles of roofs and long
manes of rain leave traces on my window,

when the last leaves let go, let go,
have *all* let go, and it's almost winter again —
don't remember my birthday.

Give me another one: let it be in May —
sated, lit: the month my children were born —
but not in November, gray-gorged

as the morning when I first gasped,
un-welcomed by my parents. Forty years later,
to the day, I closed the casket at last

on my father's bloated face, his white
mane slicked back — I almost stroked it —
no one with me

at the Antwerp crematory: my mother
too busy planning the funeral reception, and he
had no family. Not a leaf was

left on the old cemetery oaks, even
the wind had nothing to hang onto, so it
slapped the ashes into the rain that soaked

the fur coat my mother had forced me
to wear: *Do it for me, look like a lady for once.*
But no one was there to see me except for the funeral

       employees, eager to get it over with:
Belgium was playing Germany at soccer that day.
So let's say I was born in the heart of May,

       leaves alive with rain, oaks in the park
freckling benches with mellow shades.
Send me a card then, or take me

       out to a sidewalk café, and let's
not talk too much. That would be plenty,
that would be enough.

IT HAD TO BE YOU

"It had to be you . . ." Always the same
refrain he whistles at night, over and over,
from the stoop of his house across the street.
He lives alone, tousled, arthritic, small
curtains shut with a safety pin. On rainy days
he places a wandering Jew on the window sill, looks

up at it as he leaves the house, and — again — looks
up before turning the corner, wearing the same
beret and coat. Where does he spend his days
while the rain slakes his plant? Over
what desk or counter does he fray his life's small
cloth before coming back to our street

always around six? As soon as he turns the street
corner he does it again — *Jesus!* — looks
up at his window and plant, a small
gloss of dust and drizzle on its leaves. The same-
ness of it all, as he appears at the window, bends over
the plant, checks the soil, brings it in. Days,

months of these lost gestures. Days
behind that window facing Barrow Street:
ratty, dull. To whom, to what does he whistle, over
and again *It had to be you?* When he looks
up at his plant, or carries it in, did he have the same
gestures for a woman once? Was nothing small

then as she waited by their window, their small
curtains white and starched? Their days
melodic with the tunes he whistled, the same
ones, from the corner of Barrow Street?
This is what I need to believe: there were looks
of envy for them when he wrapped a shawl over

her shoulders as they sat on their stoop; that over
them the same street lamp threw its small
fortunes of light. So that now, when he looks

up at his wandering Jew, it's her he sees, their days
predictable, passive as this street.
And that this is all he needs — to remember the same.

AWE

for the veins on a woman's hands today: their
swells and curves and how inside those

narrow blue rills brilliant twirls of DNA
whirled while she sold tickets

for boat-rides on the Hudson. Then the ride:
the sky so clear, so frayed by concrete, glass,

planes, and the river thick with barges,
cruise ships and tugboats, docks clinging to her banks —

　　　that great, wide-hipped mother of a river.

And I belong to her as the boat glides
past old pier-poles sticking out like broken ribs,

riding her swells then sinking back
into her again with that languorous and deep

rocking I loved in the Scheldt river
a half century ago

　　　— how I needed that river too —

already then longing to be taken away,
taken along, yearning for

a mother, a place, anything to belong to

as Antwerp's steeples clanged to ships leaving,
leaving — leaving me behind. But this ride,

      this ten-bucks-wave-rocker-of-a-ride

is mine, and so is this million-windowed city,
trashed, ashed and gleaming, too busy

destroying then rebuilding herself to watch
the Hudson and me at the end of our journeys —

resilient and willing.

NOTE SLIPPED UNDER HIS DOOR

Could we talk about it again later?

Perhaps after turning off the lights?

Let's start by agreeing about

something first, and be furious

together, but at the terrifying news

or impossible weather.

But could we talk again?

I'll say I'm sorry first.

AT SAVAGE RIVER LODGE

Only the trees
  are raining now —

the storm passed
  through the forest

like a night shiver
  and was gone.

Out of the dark and into it, the August sizzle of crickets.

Wrapped in a blanket,
  I sit on the deck

of my one-room cabin.
  Twenty yards away, yours.

We're wise enough to know confinement sets us apart.

Earlier tonight,
  we feasted a friend

with other friends, the evening
  ample and kind.

I'm pensively dizzy with it,
        and would probably have

slipped into my usual solitary considerations,

had you not turned on
        a light in your cabin

its glow barely
        visible through the low

branches of an oak. So I
        quietly tiptoed closer

to your window, barefoot
        on gravel and grass,

and watched you be alone, not four feet away from me.

Everything you did
        was unsurprising, familiar —

you already seemed
        distant, self-contained.

And I suddenly felt
        I was no longer there,

while you went about your life without me.

What else was there
        to do for me but to look

away and walk
        back into the dark?

FRIENDS,

this is the viscous heart I hide from you:
gnashing, polluted, hooked to my ribs
like a burr, stuck there and stinging,
and it's only 4:14 in the morning.

Those sudden shudders my waking alarm,
then the daily discipline of shutting away that heart,
shambling through the house, touching things,
stroking their shapes as if it could help me

not be the Bad Sower's daughter each morning:
the pit from a seed he sowed and left to parch,
and no crows would feed on it. So I lived. I don't
want to explain this further, I'm done with it.

But this for you: on the days I hold your books,
read your letters, recall a gaze, the delicate
dangle of an earring, or the throwing
back of a head in laughter,

it's you seeding the first beat into the heart
I open. And as the sun heaves daylight
into the parched tree by my window,
and rats burrow away, when pigeons come

down to feed on dust and pizza crusts, I thrum
the lit syllables of your names on my sill with all
ten fingers, typing them firmly into the brick,
and counting their beats, counting their beats.

NIGHT

Lights go off, one by one, in buildings
across the street. There's something

solemn about this — the lone
drone of cars and cabs

an urban lullaby to shut windows.

Pull the sheet over this day, subway driver,
torah reader, birthday girl, pimp.

Pull the sheet, soldier's mother, corpse
dresser, drunk man's bride.

Sleep my daughter. Sleep my son,

and sleep Jeremiah Smith: the newborn
he delivered in a charity ward today. Sleep.

Wrap a wing around the orphan,
the hungry woman, the caged man.

Shut your eyes, face your walls, the scythe's

blade is tilting toward the earth — so
sleep for the one who knows horror,

or the one who dares speak in any god's name.

Don't listen to the clockmaker: he's setting
the alarm. Sleep until it rings — sleep

toward the waking and the windowless night.

NOTES & ACKNOWLEDGMENTS

Page 19: in the third sonnet of "The River's Mouth, the Boat, the Undertow" I translated *"The passing clouds, over there ... over there ... the marvelous clouds"* from the prose poem "L'Etranger" by Charles Baudelaire. This same line in its French version starts the next sonnet.

Page 23: in the seventh sonnet of "The River's Mouth, the Boat, the Undertow" I gratefully stole:

"shrill shirts ballooning" from "To Brooklyn Bridge" by Hart Crane

"with empty hands in the murmur of the river's mouth" from "Christmas on the Hudson" by Federico Garcia Lorca

"The two greatest poetic geniuses alive meet, and what happens," as well as *"gave each other wisdom or love or even a good time"* from "On the Meeting of Garcia Lorca and Hart Crane" by Philip Levine

*

Deep gratitude to Kimiko Hahn, Steven Huff and Meg Kearney for helping me so generously with your feedback and suggestions for these poems.

For your hearts and inspiring work my thanks
to Stephen Dunn, Kristien Hemmerechts, Doug
Goetsch, Andrey Gritsman, Barbara Hurd, Brigit
Pegeen Kelly, Anne-Marie Macari, Claudia Rankine,
Martha Rhodes, Timothy Seibles, Jason Shinder,
Gerald Stern, and Ellen Bryant Voigt — lucky me.

Your affection for me, and belief in this book, are
essential to me, Carol Houck Smith. So is your
enduring friendship, Aidan; and yours, Lorna.

And here's to you, you Savage River Gang . . .

"Amour" was made to rhyme with "toujours" *only* for
you: Kurt, Mathieu & Sara, Maelle & Barry.

"Against Again" is for Kristien Hemmerechts
"The River's Mouth, the Boat, the Undertow" is for
        Kimiko Hahn
"Counted" is for Ken Braitman and Anne Bristrow
"Garage Sale" is for Ellen Bryant Voigt
"On a Bench by the Hudson" is for Martha Rhodes
"Night" is for Meg Kearney

Grateful acknowledgment is made to the editors of the following journals where many of these poems were published, sometimes in different versions:

Chatahoochee Review, The Cortland Review (online), *Crab Orchard, The Edison Literary Review, The English Record, The Florida Review, Georgia Review, Nightsun, Rattapallax, Snake Nation Review,* and *Interpoezia Anthology* (as well as *Interpoezia* online).